This BOOK and WILD RECORD belong to

WORKMAN PUBLISHING COMPANY
NEW YORK CITY

O9-ABF-189

For the exuberant and wise Suzanne Rafer
and for the kind and funny Brian Mann

Published simultaneously in Canada by Thomas Allen & Son Limited.
ISBN 978-0-7611-8992-3
Workman Publishing Company, Inc.
225 Varick Street, New York, NY 10014-4381
Manufactured in China   First Printing August 2017
10 9 8 7 6 5 4 3 2 1

100% of the royalties for this songbook/CD set will go to Paul Newman's
THE HOLE IN THE WALL GANG CAMP
a remarkable source of joy for children and families
coping with serious illnesses.

HOLEINTHEWALLGANG.ORG

CONTENTS

PART ONE
Look While You Listen

TRACK 1

Dance It Out

I don't want to make it complicated.
   I'm not gonna let it take me down.
If the world is getting me frustrated,
  let me, oh let me hear that sound.

So I can...

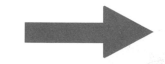

Dance it out. **DANCE! IT! OUT!**
I'm gonna dance it out. **DANCE! IT! OUT!**
I've got to dance it out.

Whoa oo-oh, oo-oh-oh!
EVERY SINGLE TROUBLE
FALLS AWAY-AY-AY!

DANCE TO PAGE 40 FOR NOTATION & ALL THE LYRICS!

TRACK
2

Tyrannosaurus Funk

Tiny little arms.
Great big head.
So many teeth,
and a heavy tread.
White T-shirt.
Rayon slacks.
Black. Frame. Glasses.
These are the facts.

I look in the mirror and what do I see? King of the World looking back at me—T. REX.

Yeah, say it again now.

TYRANNO-SAURUS REX!

TYRANNO-SAURUS REX!

T. Rex. Tyrannosaur. Tyrannosaur. Oh, yes.

I like this beat. Catchy. It's catchy! Here we go...

I'M A T. REX.
GOTTA STOMP AROUND.
I'M A T. REX.
GONNA SHAKE THE GROUND.
I CAN SAY IT NOW
LIKE I SAID IT BEFORE—
NOBODY MOVES LIKE
TYRANNOSAUR!
YEAH, NOBODY
MOVES LIKE
TYRANNOSAUR!
T. REX.

STOMP ON OVER
TO PAGE 42
FOR NOTATION
& ALL THE LYRICS!

TRACK 3

Hog Wild

Away out here in the countryside,
we all like it nice and quiet.
We all take it pretty slow.

But every now and then, we really go...

HOG WILD! We're gonna move our feet.
HOG WILD! We're gonna rock that beat.

Every man, woman, chicken, and child,
come on over now 'cause we're going HOG WILD!
Come on over now 'cause we're going HOG WILD!

SKEDADDLE
TO PAGE 44
FOR NOTATION
& ALL THE LYRICS!

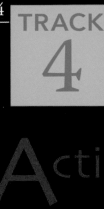

ROBOT DANCE

Activate: FUN MODE.

> ACTIVATING FUN MODE.

Hello.

> HELLO.

Robot.

> ROBOT.

Robot Dance.

5, 4, 3, 2, 1.

Rotate LEFT.

Rolling.

STOP.

Lights ON.
Blinking.

Back up.
Back up.

STOP.

Robot Dance.

ROTATE LEFT. CHECK.

ROLLING...
ROLLING...

BLINKING.
BLINKING.

YOU KNOW IT. YOU KNOW IT.

Swivel Function, Level 5.

LEVEL 5. CHECK.

Activate:
Twist.
Twist.
Twist
and Shout.
Twist
and Shout.

SHOUT!

SHOUT!

STOP

ROLL TO PAGE 46
FOR NOTATION
& ALL THE LYRICS!

TRACK 5

Ducks in a Row

Well, this crazy mad planet keeps a-turning around.
You're right side up, then you're upside down.
I don't like to tell you what you already know,
but you're gonna do better with your Ducks in a Row.

We're Ducks in a Row.
It's a wonderful sight!
Ducks in a Row.
Yeah, we move just right.

You can take it fast.

You can take it slow.

You can take it any way with your Ducks in a Row!

STROLL TO PAGE 48 FOR NOTATION & ALL THE LYRICS!

CITY

City. City, City. CITY! City, City.
Bright lights all around.
So many people and so much sound.
City. City, City. CITY! Pretty City.

Slivers of sky. Dazzle and glare.
Everybody rushing, but I don't know where.

City. City, City. CITY! City, City.

Nothing but commotion
in the day or the dark.
Way too many cars
and there's
nowhere to park.
Steel-hard buildings,
impossibly tall.
You cannot resist
the siren call
of the City. City, City!
CITY!!!
City, City!

GRAB A TAXI TO
PAGE 50
FOR NOTATION
& ALL THE LYRICS!

TRACK
7

C.A.T.

I sleep in the sun. I bat things around.
    I **POUNCE** out of nowhere.
I move with no sound.
I'm known for my grace and my curiosity.
No doubt about it,
    I'm a
    C.A.T.
    That's "cat."
    C.A.T.
    That's "cat."

FELINEWAY & Co

I love to leap,
and I like
high places.

The Sound and the Furry
The Poems of Catullus
The POWER of MEOW
A TALE OF TWO KITTES
The Great Catsby

I know how to
locate
the
unknown
spaces.

A sudden **LOUD NOISE**
will cause me to scram.

I don't enjoy surprises.
That's the Way. I. Am.
I'm a cat.
C.A.T. That's "cat."
C.A.T. That's "cat."
Yeah,

  spells "cat."

SLINK TO PAGE 52
FOR NOTATION
& ALL THE LYRICS!

And Oh I Love You So

Y ou've got a
cool way of talking
and a wonderful smile.
And Oh I Love You So!
We go out walking
for a little while.
And Oh I Love You So!

I don't care about
any old weather
whenever we're spending
time together.
It's the way you think,
and the way you are.
And Oh
I Love You So!
And Oh
I Love You So!

When I hear your name, it's a beautiful sound.
And Oh I Love You So!
Your gentle voice can turn me around.
And Oh I Love You So!
It makes me happy when I hear you sing.

Whenever you laugh, it's the greatest thing.
There's not a better friend that could ever be found.

And Oh I Love You So!
And Oh I Love You So!

JITTERBUG WITH ME
OVER TO PAGE 54
FOR NOTATION
& ALL THE LYRICS!

TRACK 9

Swing Thing

It's a Swing Thing. I don't know how it started.
It's a Swing Thing. I don't know where it goes.

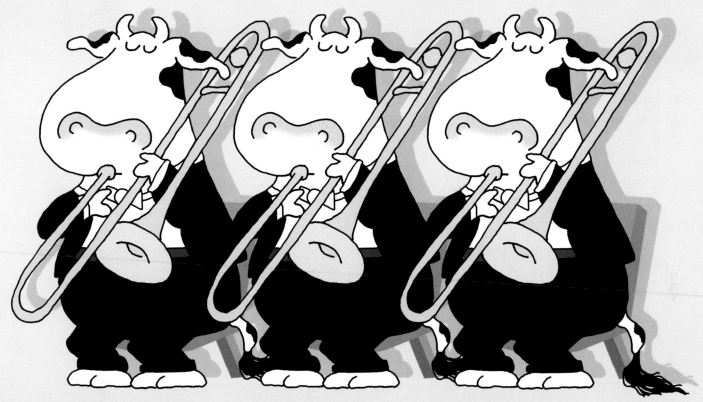

It's a Swing Thing. If you're ever downhearted,
let the music take you like nobody knows.

Whenever you've got to lose the blues,
it's a whole lot better if you
move your shoes.

RAT RACE

*AND IT'S A BEAUTIFUL DAY FOR RACING RATS,
BROADCAST LIVE FROM RIVERTOWN FLATS.*
AND THEY'RE OFF!

A hundred rats take off in a pack.
I don't see anyone hanging back.
That's Rat 17 who's setting the pace.
It's going to be an exciting race.
Now Rat Number 5   has taken the lead,
    but Rat 46 is   picking up speed.
Coming up fast   in the outside lane,
  we've got Rat Number 8, "The Hurricane."

RAT RACE! RUNNING IN CIRCLES.
RAT RACE! 'ROUND AND 'ROUND.
WHY THEY DO IT, WE DON'T KNOW.
LET 'EM LOOSE AND WATCH 'EM GO!

Let 'em loose and watch 'em go!

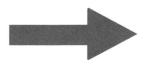

As the rats approach the
switchback turn,
the leading rats show
no concern.
But out of nowhere,
rocket-fast,
Rat 66 comes blazing past!
Gaining on the inside: 92.
Now Rat 38
is barreling through.
Rat Number 5 kicks into play,
and it's neck and neck on the straightaway!

IT'S NECK AND NECK ON THE STRAIGHTAWAY!
THE CROWD GOES WILD!

HIGHTAIL IT TO
PAGE 58
FOR NOTATION
& ALL THE LYRICS!

EASY

Easy.
Keep it light as a breeze.
Easy. Make it
slow as you please.
Easy. It's a
walk in the park.
Easy.
Easy.

Easy. You can slow it down.
Easy. You can turn it around.
Easy. Take your own sweet time.
Easy. Yeah, easy.

Easy, like a summer smile.
Easy. Come and stroll a while.
Easy is the way it should be.
Make it easy as A, B, C, D, Easy.

MOSEY TO PAGE 60
FOR NOTATION
& ALL THE LYRICS!

PART TWO
Sing and Play Along

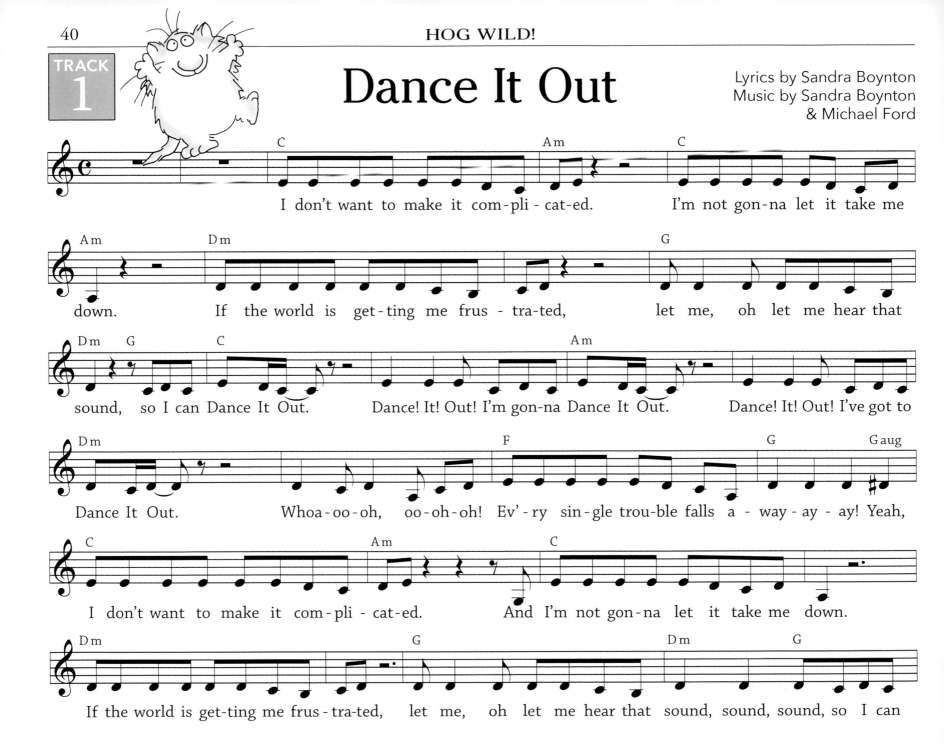

Dance It Out

Lyrics by Sandra Boynton
Music by Sandra Boynton
& Michael Ford

I don't want to make it com-pli-cat-ed. I'm not gon-na let it take me down. If the world is get-ting me frus-tra-ted, let me, oh let me hear that sound, so I can Dance It Out. Dance! It! Out! I'm gon-na Dance It Out. Dance! It! Out! I've got to Dance It Out. Whoa-oo-oh, oo-oh-oh! Ev'-ry sin-gle trou-ble falls a-way-ay-ay! Yeah, I don't want to make it com-pli-cat-ed. And I'm not gon-na let it take me down. If the world is get-ting me frus-tra-ted, let me, oh let me hear that sound, sound, sound, so I can

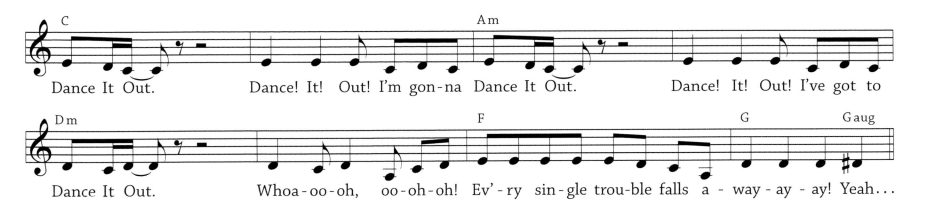

Dance It Out.   Dance! It! Out! I'm gon-na Dance It Out.   Dance! It! Out! I've got to

Dance It Out.   Whoa-oo-oh,   oo-oh-oh! Ev'-ry sin-gle trou-ble falls a - way-ay - ay! Yeah...

. . . it doesn't have to be so complicated.
And I won't ever let it take me down, down, down.
When the world is getting me frustrated,
let me let me let me hear that sound.

Whatcha gonna do about it? Whatcha gonna do?
Say, whatcha gonna do about it? Whatcha gonna do?
Say, whatcha gonna do about it? Whatcha gonna do?
Yeah, I'm just gonna dance, dance, dance, dance,
Dance It Out.

And I will Dance It Out. Dance! It! Out!
I'm gonna Dance It Out. Dance! It! Out!
I've got to Dance It Out.
Dance! Dance! Whoa oh-oh,
every single trouble falls away, ay, ay! Yeah—

Everybody dance now. Everybody dance.
Everybody dance now. Everybody dance.
Everybody dance now. Everybody dance.
Everybody dance now. Dance! Dance! Dance!

Yeah—
Dance It Out. Dance! It! Out!
We're gonna Dance It Out. Dance! It! Out!
You've got to Dance It Out.
Whoa-oo-oh, oo-oh-oh!
Every single trouble falls away, ay, ay!

Yeah—Dance It Out. Dance! It! Out!
We're gonna Dance It Out. Dance! It! Out!
You've got to Dance It Out. Dance! It! Out!
We're gonna Dance It Out.
Dance, dance, dance.
You've got to Dance It Out. Dance! It! Out!
Come on and Dance It Out. Dance! It! Out!
You've got to Dance It Out. Dance! It! Out!
We're gonna Dance It Out. Dance! It! Out!
You've got to Dance It Out.
Dance it! Dance it!
Every single trouble falls away, ay, ay, ay,
ay, ay, ay, ay, ay, ay, ay, ay,
yeah, yeah, yeah, yeah, yeah, yeah . . .

Tyrannosaurus Funk

Lyrics by
Sandra Boynton
Music by
Sandra Boynton
& Michael Ford

TINY LITTLE ARMS. GREAT BIG HEAD.
SO MANY TEETH, AND A HEAVY TREAD.
WHITE T-SHIRT. RAYON SLACKS.
BLACK. FRAME. GLASSES. THESE ARE THE FACTS.
I LOOK IN THE MIRROR AND WHAT DO I SEE?
KING OF THE WORLD LOOKING BACK AT ME.
T. REX. *(TYRANNOSAURUS REX!)* YEAH,
SAY IT AGAIN NOW. *(TYRANNOSAURUS REX!)*
T. REX TYRANNOSAUR. TYRANNOSAUR. OH, YES.

(I LIKE THIS BEAT. CATCHY.
IT'S CATCHY! HERE WE GO...)

CHORUS

I'm a T. REX. Got-ta stomp a-round. I'm a T. REX. Gon-na shake the ground. I can say it now like I

said it be-fore— No-bo-dy moves like Ty-ran-no-saur! Yeah, no-bo-dy moves like Ty-ran-no-saur! T. REX.

NOBODY MOVES LIKE TYRANNOSAUR.

I'M A FRIENDLY GUY. LIKE TO SHAKE YOUR HAND.
BUT I CAN'T REACH. YOU UNDERSTAND.
I'M BIGGER THAN LIFE. (NO SPECIAL EFFECTS!)
I CAN CALL YOU WHATEVER. YOU CAN CALL ME REX—T. REX.

[CHORUS]

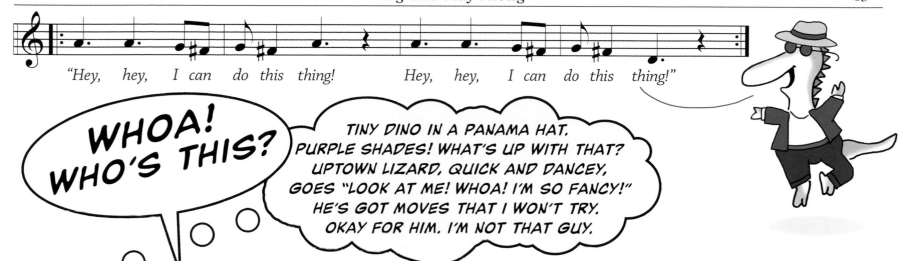

"Hey, hey, I can do this thing! Hey, hey, I can do this thing!"

WHOA! WHO'S THIS?

TINY DINO IN A PANAMA HAT.
PURPLE SHADES! WHAT'S UP WITH THAT?
UPTOWN LIZARD, QUICK AND DANCEY,
GOES "LOOK AT ME! WHOA! I'M SO FANCY!"
HE'S GOT MOVES THAT I WON'T TRY.
OKAY FOR HIM. I'M NOT THAT GUY.

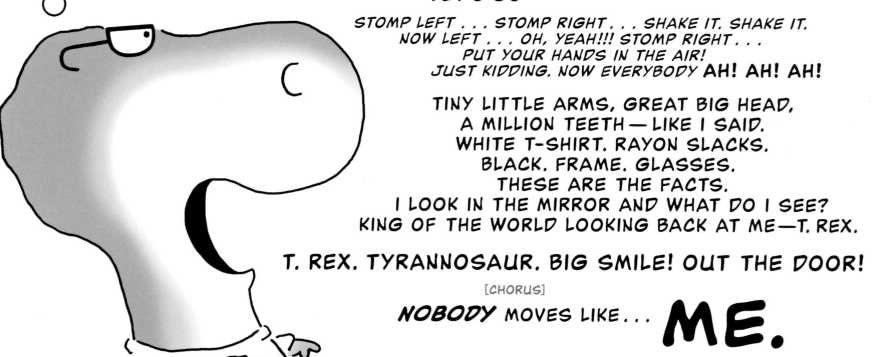

I'M A T. REX, TYRANNOSAUR! I'M A T. REX! GOTTA SHAKE THE FLOOR!
I'M A T. REX! GOTTA STOMP AROUND! I'M A T. REX! GOTTA SHAKE THE GROUND!
LET'S GO—

STOMP LEFT . . . STOMP RIGHT . . . SHAKE IT. SHAKE IT.
NOW LEFT . . . OH, YEAH!!! STOMP RIGHT . . .
PUT YOUR HANDS IN THE AIR!
JUST KIDDING. NOW EVERYBODY AH! AH! AH!

TINY LITTLE ARMS, GREAT BIG HEAD,
A MILLION TEETH—LIKE I SAID.
WHITE T-SHIRT. RAYON SLACKS.
BLACK. FRAME. GLASSES.
THESE ARE THE FACTS.
I LOOK IN THE MIRROR AND WHAT DO I SEE?
KING OF THE WORLD LOOKING BACK AT ME—T. REX.

T. REX. TYRANNOSAUR. BIG SMILE! OUT THE DOOR!

[CHORUS]

NOBODY MOVES LIKE . . . **ME.**

TRACK 3

Hog Wild

Lyrics and Music by Sandra Boynton

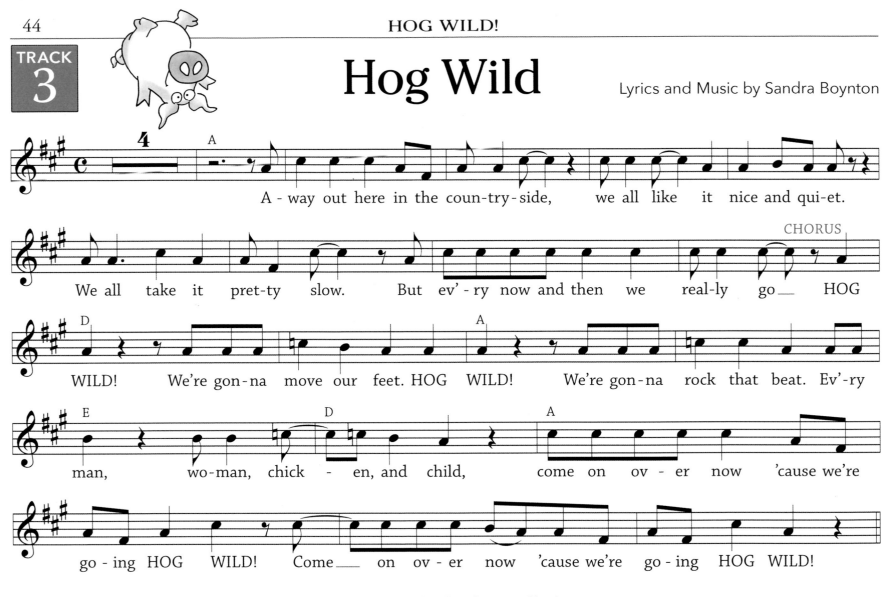

A - way out here in the coun-try-side, we all like it nice and qui-et.

We all take it pret-ty slow. But ev'-ry now and then we real-ly go___ HOG

CHORUS

WILD! We're gon-na move our feet. HOG WILD! We're gon-na rock that beat. Ev'-ry

man, wo-man, chick - en, and child, come on ov - er now 'cause we're

go - ing HOG WILD! Come___ on ov - er now 'cause we're go - ing HOG WILD!

Hey, Everybody, I'm a-tellin' you
dancing is the thing to do.
I don't know what we're waiting for.
I think we ought to go just a little bit more

[CHORUS]

If you want to have some fun, here's the way for everyone.
Find out what it's all about. Get a little crazy and shake it out!

HOG WILD!
We're gonna move our feet.
HOG WILD!
We're gonna rock that beat.
Every man, woman, chicken, and child,
come on over now 'cause we're going HOG WILD!
Come on over now 'cause we're going HOG WILD!

Oh yeah!

Here we go—

HOG WILD! We're gonna move our feet.
HOG WILD! We're gonna rock that beat.
HOG WILD! We're gonna dance all night.
HOG WILD! Till the sky is light.
Every man, woman, chicken, and child,
come on over now 'cause we're going HOG WILD!
Come on over now 'cause we're going HOG WILD!

[Repeat CHORUS, and then add:]
Come on over now 'cause we're going HOG WILD!
You know what? HOG WILD!
You know what? HOG WILD!
You know what? HOG WILD!
You know what? HOG WILD!
You know what? HOG WILD!
You know what? HOG WILD!
You know what? HOG WILD!
You know what? HOG WILD!
You know what? HOG WILD!
You know what? HOG WILD!
You know what? HOG WILD!
You know what? HOG WILD!

[Pause for dramatic effect.]

You know what? HOG WILD! You know what?
HOG WILD! HOG WILD! HOG WILD!

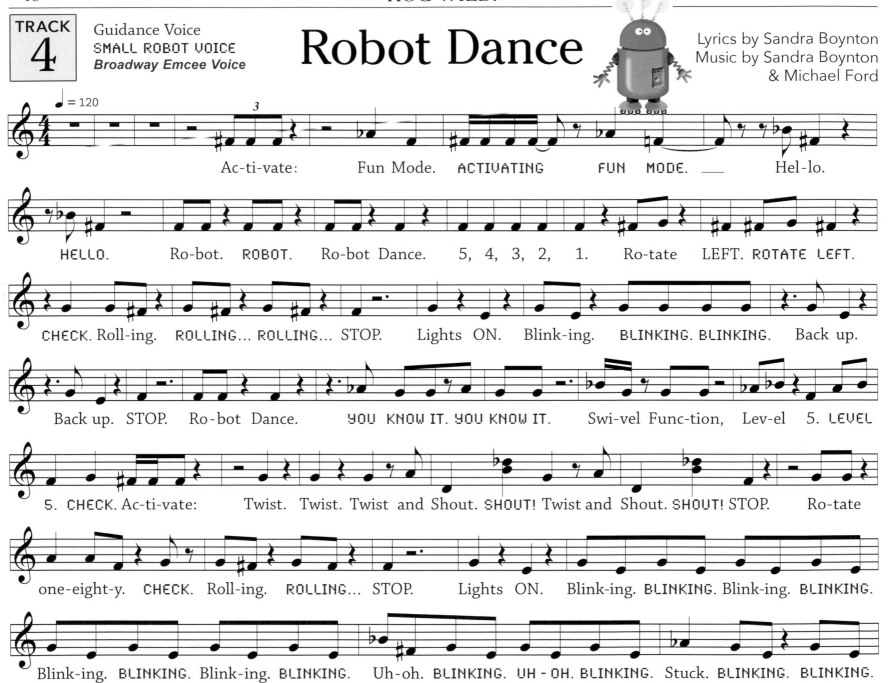

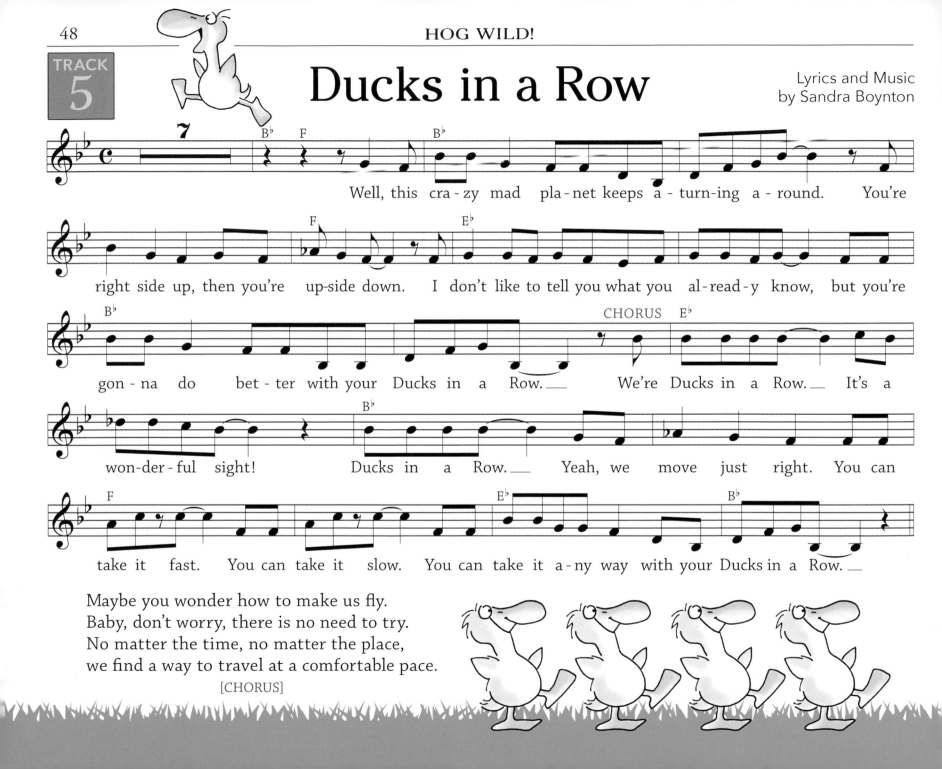

Ducks in a Row

Lyrics and Music
by Sandra Boynton

Well, this cra-zy mad pla-net keeps a-turn-ing a-round. You're right side up, then you're up-side down. I don't like to tell you what you al-read-y know, but you're gon-na do bet-ter with your Ducks in a Row.___ We're Ducks in a Row.___ It's a won-der-ful sight! Ducks in a Row.___ Yeah, we move just right. You can take it fast. You can take it slow. You can take it a-ny way with your Ducks in a Row.___

Maybe you wonder how to make us fly.
Baby, don't worry, there is no need to try.
No matter the time, no matter the place,
we find a way to travel at a comfortable pace.

[CHORUS]

You count—

1 2 3 4 5 6 7 8 9 10 AND 11

ZIP! ZOP! ZAM! AND WHAT DO YOU KNOW? ALL OF A SUDDEN, YOU'VE GOT **DUCKS** IN A ROW!

Aw, whenever you're feeling just a little bit blue,
I think you understand what you've gotta do—
Find yourself a place in our perfect line,
and just start dancing, and WOO! So fine.

Ducks in a Row. Yeah, we do The Stroll.
Ducks in a Row. Now we Rock and Roll.
We can take it fast. We can take it slow.
We can take it any way 'cause we're Ducks in a Row!

Yeah, this crazy mad planet keeps a-turning around.
You're right-side up, then you're upside down.
I don't like to tell you what you already know, but
you're gonna do better with your Ducks in a Row.
You're gonna do better with your Ducks in a Row.
Mmm, you're gonna do better with your
Ducks in a Row!

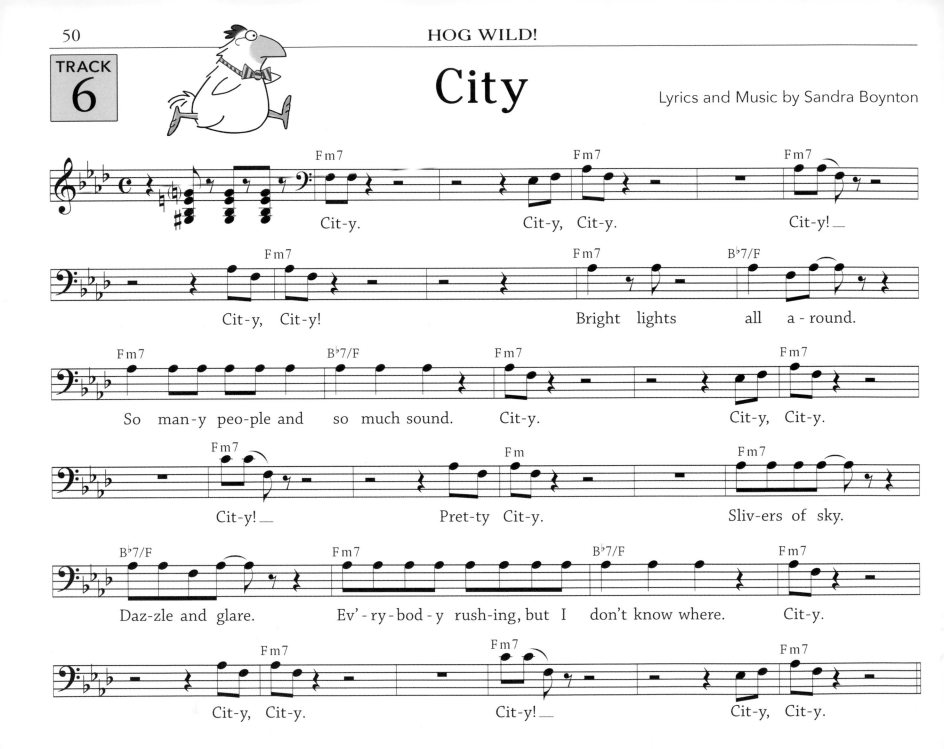

Nothing but commotion in the day or the dark.
Way too many cars and there's nowhere to park.
Steel-hard buildings, impossibly tall.
You cannot resist the siren call of the City! City, City! CITY! City, City!

Yeah, bright lights all around.
So many people and so much sound.
Slivers of sky. Dazzle and glare.
Everybody rushing, but I
don't know where.

City!
City, City!
CITY!
Pretty City!
Yeah, take me
to the City.

We go go go in a kind of a trance,
connecting to the rhythm, and you feel the dance of the City.
Feel the dance of the City. Feel the dance of the City.
Feel the dance. Feel the dance of the City.
Feel the Dance. Feel the Dance. Feel the Dance.
I love the City.
City.

C.A.T.

Lyrics and Music by Sandra Boynton

TRACK 7

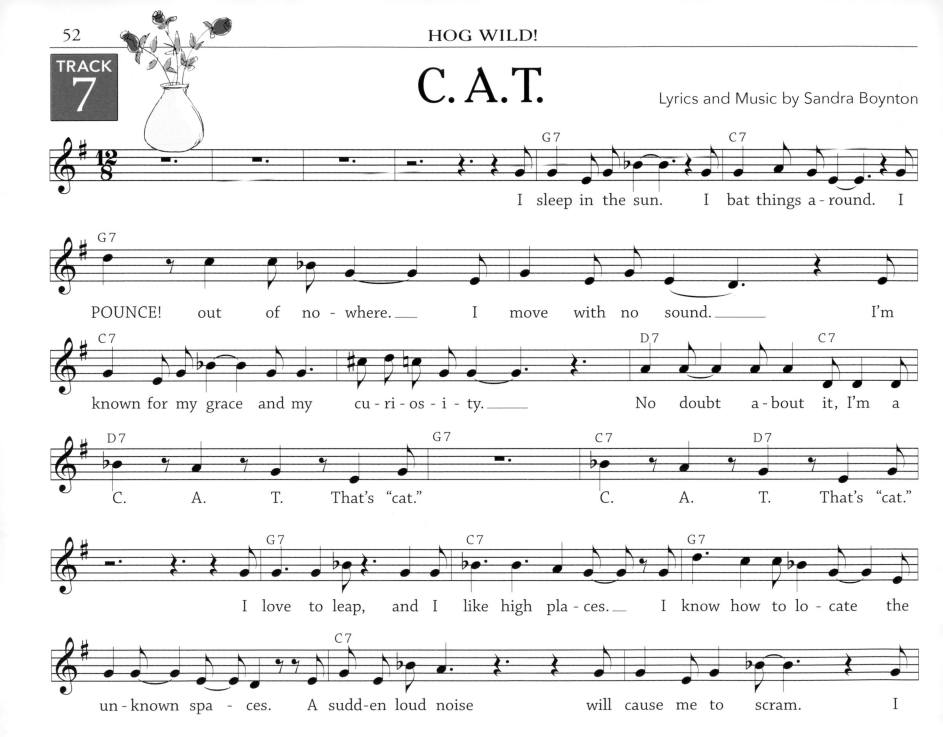

I sleep in the sun. I bat things a-round. I

POUNCE! out of no-where. I move with no sound. I'm

known for my grace and my cu-ri-os-i-ty. No doubt a-bout it, I'm a

C. A. T. That's "cat." C. A. T. That's "cat."

I love to leap, and I like high pla-ces. I know how to lo-cate the

un-known spa-ces. A sudd-en loud noise will cause me to scram. I

Now no two cats are exactly the same.
We each have a style and a secret name.
We drift like a dream, then off like a shot.
We choose to knock things over
just to shake things up. Like a cat.
C. A. T. That's "cat."
Yeah, C. A. T. That's "cat."
That's "cat."

I sleep in the sun.
I bat things around.
I pounce out of nowhere.
I move with no sound.
I'm known for my grace
and my curiosity.
No doubt about it.
I'm a . . . CAT.

And Oh I Love You So

Lyrics and Music
by Sandra Boynton

You've got a cool way of tal-king and a won-der-ful smile. And

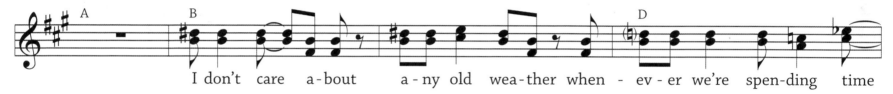

Oh I Love You So! We go out wal-king for a lit-tle while. And Oh I Love You So!

I don't care a-bout a-ny old wea-ther when-ev-er we're spen-ding time

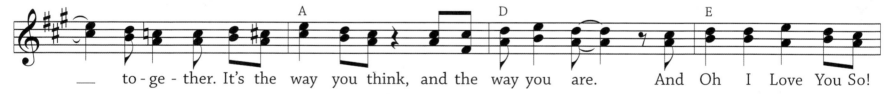

__ to-ge-ther. It's the way you think, and the way you are. And Oh I Love You So!

And Oh I Love You So! When I hear your name, it's a beau-ti-ful sound. And

Oh I Love You So! Your gen-tle voice can turn me a-round. And Oh I Love You So!

It makes me hap - py when I hear you sing. When - ev - er you laugh, it's the

great-est thing. There's not a bet-ter friend that could ev-er be found. And Oh I Love You So!

And Oh I Love You So! I could ne-ver ex-plain what you mean to me.

How can I tell you all the things I see?___ You're nat'-ral-ly kind and brave

___ and smart. Ev' - ry - thing you do just touch-es my heart.

You've got a cool way of talking and
a wonderful smile. And Oh I Love You So!
We go out walking for a little while.
And Oh I Love You So!
I don't care about any old weather
as long as we spend some time together.
It's the way you think, and the way you are.
And Oh I Love You So! You know I love you so!
("Let's dance." "All right.")
I could never explain what you mean to me.
How can I tell you all the things I see?
You're naturally kind. Brave and smart.
Everything you do just touches my heart.

I like the way that you hold my hand.
And Oh I Love You So!
I like the way that you understand.
And Oh I Love You So!
There are so many things
that I don't know,
but I sure do know I love you so.
I sure do know I love you so.
And Oh I Love You So! And Oh I Love You So!
And Oh I Love You So! You know I love you so!
And Oh I Love You So!
And Oh I Love You So!
And Oh I Love You So-oo-oh!

TRACK 9

Swing Thing

Lyrics by Sandra Boynton
Music by Sandra Boynton & Michael Ford

It's a Swing Thing. I don't know how it start-ed. It's a Swing Thing. I don't

know where it goes. It's a Swing Thing. If you're ev-er down-heart-ed, __ let the mu-sic take you like

no-bod-y knows. Oh, it's a Swing Thing. I don't know how it start-ed. It's a Swing Thing. I don't

know where it goes. But it's a Swing Thing. If you're ev-er down-heart-ed, __ let the mu-sic take you like

no-bod-y knows. When - ev-er you've got to lose __ the blues, it's a

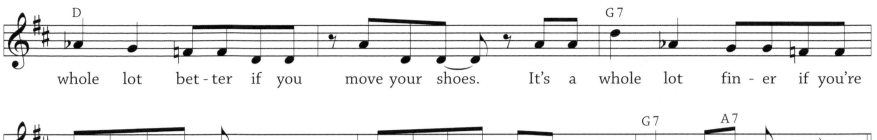

whole   lot   bet - ter   if   you   move your   shoes.   It's   a   whole   lot   fin - er   if   you're

tak - ing   a   chance.   You've got - ta   give   it   o - ver   and   join   the   dance.

[I don't know how it started.
I don't know where it goes.]
Swing Thing.
If you're ever downhearted,
let the music take you
like nobody knows.
[Let the music take you
like nobody knows.]

[It's a Swing Thing, ah.]
How did it start?
[It's a Swing Thing, ooo.]
Where's it gonna take us?
[It's a Swing Thing.]
Oh, you can't be downhearted
if you let the music take you
like nobody knows.

Ah, whenever you've got to
lose the blues,
it's a whole lot better if you
move the shoes.

It's a whole lot finer
if you're taking a chance.
[Give it up! Give it up! Give it up!
Give it over to a—]
Swing Thing. *[Swing!]*

Uh, you gotta swing it. *[Swing it.]* Swing it.
[Uh, uh! You gotta swing it.]

Swing Thing.
Give it a chance. A chance!

[It's that] Swing—
Don't know how it started.
[It's that] Swing—
Goin' where it goes.
[Feel that—]
No, you can't be downhearted
if you let the music take you.
Let the music take you.
Let the music take you . . .
like nobody knows.
Nobody knows.
It's a Swing Thing. *[Swing Thing.]*
Swing Thing. *[Swing Thing.]*
Swing Thing. *[Swing Thing.]*
Swing Thing. *[Swing Thing.]*
Swing . . . *[Swing, swing.]*
Thing.
Ooo!
It's a Swing Thing.

RAT RACE

Lyrics and Music
by Sandra Boynton

**AND IT'S A BEAUTIFUL DAY FOR RACING RATS,
BROADCAST LIVE FROM RIVERTOWN FLATS. *AND THEY'RE OFF!***

A hundred rats take off in a pack. I don't see anyone hanging back.
That's Rat 17 who's setting the pace. It's going to be an exciting race.
Now Rat Number 5 has taken the lead, but Rat 46 is picking up speed.
Coming up fast in the outside lane,
we've got Rat Number 8,
"The Hurricane."

CHORUS

Rat Race! Run-ning in cir-cles. Rat Race! 'Round and 'round. Why they do it, we don't know. Let 'em loose and watch 'em go!

Rat Race! Run-ning in cir-cles. Rat Race! 'Round and 'round. Why they do it, we don't know. Let 'em loose and watch 'em go!

Rat Race! Run-ning in cir-cles. Rat Race! 'Round and 'round. Why they do it, we don't know. Let 'em loose and watch 'em go!

Let 'em loose and watch 'em go!
As the rats approach the switchback turn,
the leading rats show no concern.
But out of nowhere, rocket-fast, Rat 66 comes blazing past.
Gaining on the inside: 92. Now Rat 38 is barreling through.
Rat Number 5 kicks into play,
and it's neck and neck on the straightaway!

IT'S NECK AND NECK ON THE STRAIGHTAWAY! THE CROWD GOES WILD!

[CHORUS]

Just let 'em loose and watch 'em go!
**IF YOU'RE JUST JOINING US HERE TODAY, THE GREAT RAT RACE IS UNDER WAY.
IT'S A PERFECT DAY FOR RACING RATS, BROADCAST LIVE FROM RIVERTOWN FLATS.**

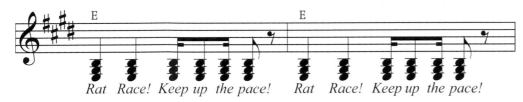

Rat Race! Keep up the pace! Rat Race! Keep up the pace!

Last year's winner has fallen back.
He's lost somewhere in the middle of the pack.
Rat Number 5 is hugging the rail.
Rat 78 is on his tail. Coming up fast, Rat 99,
with Rat 13 running close behind.
Now it's straight uphill, heading into the maze.
Some of them won't come out for days.

**NOW THEY'RE HEADING INTO THE RAT MAZE.
I'VE GOT NO IDEA WHO'S IN THE LEAD.**

*Rats in a maze!
Running like crazy.
Rats in a maze! So confused.
Nobody knows which way to go.
A hundred rats running to and fro, and to and fro…*

…because most of the rats don't have a clue.
But a few of the rats have made it through.
Rat 19 is good to go. 2 and 7 are looking slow.
Rat 66 pulls out in front.
Whoa! Rat 29 is out of the hunt!
As they enter the turn, it's beginning to rain,
and there seems to be a rabbit that we can't explain.

*Rat Race! Running in circles.
Rat Race! 'Round and 'round.
Why they do it, we don't know.
Let 'em loose and watch 'em go, go, go…*

**WE'RE IN THE HOME STRETCH!
IT'S A SPRINT TO THE FINISH!**

*Rat Race! Pick up the pace!
Rat Race! Pick up the pace!*

26 is in the lead. 44 is gaining speed.
Rat 88 kicks into gear,
6 and 7 are incredibly near.
40 moves into second place.
Everybody's going at record pace.
With flapping tails and flying fur,
the entire track is just a blur!
Rat Race! Rat Race!

**WAIT! THERE SEEMS TO BE NO FINISH LINE…
I GUESS WE'RE GOING TILL THE END OF TIME.**

Rat Race! Rat Race! Rat Race! Rat Race!

Easy

Lyrics by Sandra Boynton
Music by Sandra Boynton & Michael Ford

TRACK 11

Eas-y. Keep it light as a breeze. Eas-y. Make it slow as you please.

Eas-y. It's a walk in the park. Eas-y. Eas-y. Eas-y. You can

slow it down. Eas-y. You can turn it a-round. Eas-y. Take your own sweet time.

Eas-y. Yeah, eas-y. Eas-y.___ Like a sum-mer smile. Eas-y.___ Come and

stroll a while. Eas-y___ is the way it should be. Make it eas - y as A, B, C, D,

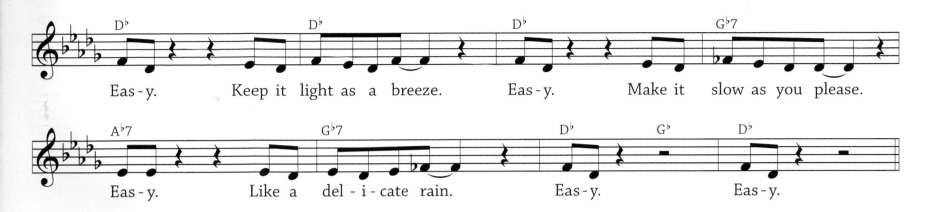

Eas-y. Keep it light as a breeze. Eas-y. Make it slow as you please.

Eas-y. Like a del-i-cate rain. Eas-y. Eas-y.

Easy is the way it should be.
Easy. You can take it from me.
Easy. And additionally, I'd like to
make it easy as 1, 2, 3, for it's easy.

Easy is the way it should be.
Easy. You can take it from me.
Easy. For simplicity's sake.
Make it free and easy. It's a piece of cake.

You know it's
easy. You can slow it down.
Easy. You can turn it around.
Easy. Take your own sweet time.
Easy. Easy.

It's easy. Easy. So easy. Easy.
Make it easy. Easy.
Take it easy. Easy.
Go easy. Easy.

MEET THE HOG WILD SINGERS

(shown in order of appearance)

photo: SHOWTIME Brian Bowen Smith

KRISTEN BELL

Dance It Out

SAMUEL L. JACKSON

Tyrannosaurus Funk

photo: Michael Schwartz

photo: Chad Griffiths

PATRICK WILSON

Hog Wild

photo: Joan Marcus

photo: Robert Trachtenberg

LAURA LINNEY & "WEIRD AL" YANKOVIC

Robot Dance

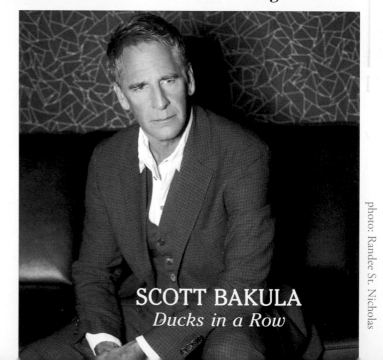

photo: Randee St. Nicholas

SCOTT BAKULA

Ducks in a Row

photo: Brandin Photography

CAITLIN McEWAN & FALLS MOUNTAIN COWBOYS *City*

photo: Jonathan Doster

photo: Ron Rinaldi

DARCY BOYNTON
C. A. T.

photo: Kristin Hoebermann

RAÚL ESPARZA & MADELEINE LODGE

And Oh I Love You So

photo: Jeremy Cowart

FIVE FOR FIGHTING
Swing Thing

photo: Susan Shacter

photo: Eric Charbonneau

STANLEY TUCCI
Rat Race

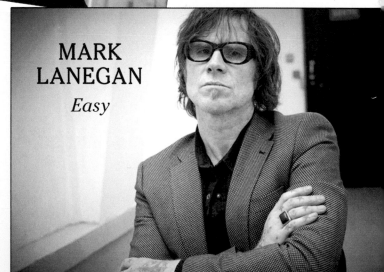

MARK LANEGAN
Easy

MEET THE MUSICIANS

FRED ELTRINGHAM
DRUMS

photo: Ulysses Salazar

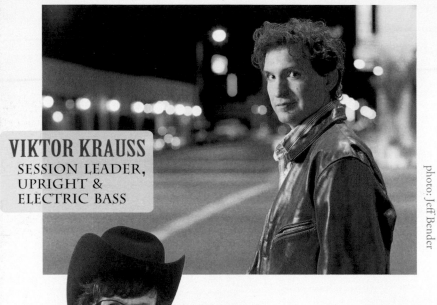

VIKTOR KRAUSS
SESSION LEADER,
UPRIGHT &
ELECTRIC BASS

photo: Jeff Bender

JIM HOKE

**KENNY
VAUGHAN**
ELECTRIC
GUITAR

MICHAEL FORD
PIANO, KEYBOARDS

photo: Lisa Haddad

PEDAL STEEL, SAXOPHONE

Dance It Out **Kristen Bell**
VOCAL RECORDED AT Henson Studios, Hollywood
ENGINEER Marc DeSisto
BAND Michael Ford, Jim Hoke
BACKUP SINGERS Beth Andrien Ford,
Darcy Boynton

Tyrannosaurus Funk **Samuel L. Jackson**
VOCAL RECORDED AT Margarita Mix, Hollywood
ENGINEER Konrad Piñon
VIRTUAL BAND Michael Ford, wearing many hats
TINY DINO IN THE PANAMA HAT John Ondrasik
BACKUP SINGERS James Creque, Sandra Boynton,
Michael Ford

Hog Wild **Patrick Wilson**
VOCAL RECORDED AT Flux Studios, NYC
ENGINEER Tom Beuchel
BAND Kenny Vaughan, Michael Ford, Viktor Krauss,
Fred Eltringham
BACKUP SINGERS Beth Andrien Ford, Darcy Boynton,
Michael Ford, Sandra Boynton

Robot Dance **Laura Linney & "Weird Al" Yankovic**
L.L. VOCAL RECORDED AT Studio Mike
ENGINEER Michael Ford
W.A.Y. VOCAL RECORDED AT Paramount Recording, Hollywood
ENGINEER Chris Tergesen
SOUND CONSTRUCTION Sandra Boynton and Michael Ford
SMALL ROBOT Sandra Boynton
BROADWAY BACKUP SINGERS Michael Ford, Sandra Boynton

Ducks in a Row **Scott Bakula**
VOCAL RECORDED AT Capitol Recording, Hollywood
ENGINEER Ira Grylack
VIRTUAL BAND Michael Ford SAXOPHONE Jim Hoke
BACKUP SINGERS Michael Ford, Michael Ford, Michael Ford

"Every man, woman, chicken, and child..."

City **Falls Mountain Cowboys & Caitlin McEwan**
Graham Stone, Keith Boynton, Devin McEwan, Michael Ford
VOCALS RECORDED AT Quad Studios, NYC
ENGINEER Jonathan Wright
EXTRA VOCAL RECORDING BY
Graham Stone at Stone Studio, Lakeville, Connecticut
SOUND COLLAGE Sandra Boynton and Michael Ford

C.A.T. **Darcy Boynton**
VOCAL RECORDED AT Studio Mike
ENGINEER Michael Ford
BAND Michael Ford, Viktor Krauss
CAT ON THE KEYS PIANO SOLO Sandra Boynton

And Oh I Love You So
Raúl Esparza & Madeleine Lodge
VOCALS RECORDED AT Quad Studios, NYC
ENGINEER Jonathan Wright
BAND Michael Ford, Viktor Krauss, Fred Eltringham

Swing Thing **Five For Fighting**
John Ondrasik, lead vocal
VOCAL RECORDED AT John's Place
ENGINEER John Ondrasik
BAND Michael Ford Virtual Orchestra
BACKUP SINGERS Olivia Ondrasik, Beth Andrien Ford

Rat Race **Stanley Tucci**
VOCAL RECORDED AT Capitol Recording, Hollywood
ENGINEER Chandler Harrod
BAND Ron Block, Kenny Vaughan, Stuart Duncan,
Russ Pahl, Viktor Krauss, Shannon Forrest
BLUEGRASS HARMONY John Stey, Charlie Roehrig, Michael Ford

Easy **Mark Lanegan**
VOCAL RECORDED AT Henson Studios, Hollywood ENGINEER Marc DeSisto
BAND Michael Ford, Jim Hoke, Fred Eltringham
SUBLIMINAL HARMONY Sandra Boynton

All recording sessions produced by Sandra Boynton
All tracks written, arranged, and mixed by Sandra Boynton & Michael Ford at Studio Mike, Nowhere, Connecticut
Instruments recorded at Southern Ground, Nashville • RECORDING ENGINEER Mike Poole
"Rat Race" instruments recorded at House of Blues, Nashville • RECORDING ENGINEER Neal Cappellino
Album mastered at Gateway Mastering, Portland, Maine • MASTERING ENGINEER Bob Ludwig

BOOK CREDITS & GENERAL THANKYOUS

A PROFOUND THANKYOU TO ALL OF THE STUNNINGLY GREAT PEOPLE AT WORKMAN PUBLISHING, INCLUDING

MY WONDROUS EDITOR **Suzanne Rafer**

OUR FEARLESS LEADER **Dan Reynolds**

PRODUCTION MASTERMIND **Doug Wolff**

INGENIOUS PUBLICITY **Selina Meere** *and* **Noreen Herits**

SUPERBLY SMART SALES AND MARKETING **Page Edmunds** *and* **Jenny Mandel**

DEVASTATINGLY COOL ART PEOPLE **Mike Vago** *and* **Paul Hanson**

SUPERVIGILANT PRODUCTION EDITOR **Jessica Rozler**

AND LOUD THANKS TO MY GREAT PRINT-READINESS TEAM

SPIFFY MUSIC ENGRAVING **Bruce Johnson**

INDEFATIGABLE PRE-PRESS **Terry Ortolani**

PAINSTAKING FILE PREP **Bob Alessi**

WITH INEXPRESSIBLE GRATITUDE FOR YOUR THOUGHTFUL AND PERFECTLY-TIMED INSPIRATION

Darcy Boynton
Keith Boynton
Pam Boynton
Helen Brandt
Jane Capecelatro
Mike Hagerman
Laura Linney
Bob *and* Gail Ludwig
Peter Lundeen
Brian Mann
Caitlin McEwan
Devin C. B. McEwan
Theo Meneau
Carla Ondrasik
Terry Ortolani
Nora *and* Bob Rivkin
Eric Stoltz
Carolan Workman
Suzanne Yankovic

WITH ABIDING APPRECIATION TO EVERY ONE OF THESE TERRIFIC ARTIST REPRESENTATIVES

Rick Baker
Kevin Gasser
Darren Gilmore
Toni Howard
Michael Katcher
Jay Levey
Tony Lipp
Brian Mann
Eli Selden
Steven Smith

. . . AND THESE SUPERB FACILITATORS

Zac Caputo
Monica Padman
Jordan Rozansky

SO MUCH GRATITUDE FOR YOUR CLEVER VIDEOGRAPHY AND YOUR INFINITE KINDNESS

Beth Andrien Ford

And thank you to my tireless friends at The Hole in the Wall Gang Camp—Jimmy Canton, Maria Gomez, Ken Alberti, Ryan Thompson, and all the many extraordinary people who participate in the Camp's visionary and far-reaching work.